The Blessing of Christmas

JOSEPH RATZINGER
(Pope Benedict XVI)

The Blessing of Christmas

Translated by Brian McNeil

IGNATIUS PRESS   SAN FRANCISCO

Chapter opening illustration: Book with the prophecy:
"Behold, a virgin shall conceive
and bear a son, and shall call his name Immanuel" (Is 7:14).
A detail from the scene of the Annunication
on the Isenheim altar by Matthias Grünewald.
Colmar, Museum Unterlinden

Original German edition:
Der Segen der Weihnacht: Meditationen
© 2005 by Libreria Editrice Vaticana, Vatican City
© 2005 by Verlag Herder, Freiburg im Breisgau

Cover art:
Adoration of the Magi (detail)
Gentile da Fabriano (1385–1427)
Uffizi, Florence, Italy
© Erich Lessing/Art Resource, New York

Cover design by Roxanne Mei Lum

© Libreria Editrice Vaticana
© 1986, 2007 by Ignatius Press, San Francisco
All rights reserved
ISBN 978-1-58617-172-8
Library of Congress Control Number 2006939357
Printed in Canada ∞

Contents

Preface

This book brings together in one volume two earlier books by Joseph Ratzinger that perfectly complement each other: *Licht, das uns leuchtet* (The light that shines upon us; 1978) and *Lob der Weihnacht* (Praise of Christmas; 1982, by Cardinal Ratzinger and Heinrich Schlier). Most of these meditations were written during Cardinal Ratzinger's time as Archbishop of Munich. They were composed for a general public in the form of sermons, radio addresses, or newspaper articles.

These two volumes were very popular but have long been out of print. They are republished here

Christ, the center of history: Cupola mosaic, ca. 1320.
Istanbul, Chora Monastery

in a single volume. They show Joseph Ratzinger, now Pope Benedict XVI, as a spiritual man who knows how to address both mind and heart.

Freiburg, July 2005
Verlag Herder

From the Author's Foreword to
Licht, das uns leuchtet
(The light that shines upon us)

The meditations presented in this short book were written on various occasions during Advent and Christmastide of 1977. I am grateful to Verlag Herder for suggesting that they should be gathered together and published in this form. They have one aim: to awaken that internal act of seeing which can perceive the truth in the words of Scripture: "The goodness and loving kindness of God our Savior [has] appeared" to us (Tit 3:4).

From the Author's Foreword to
Lob der Weihnacht
(Praise of Christmas)

From a theological point of view, Easter is the center of the Church year; but Christmas is the most profoundly human feast of faith, because it allows us to feel most deeply the humanity of God. The crib has a unique power to show us what it means to say that God wished to be "Immanuel"—a "God with us", a God whom we may address in intimate language, because he encounters us as a child. This makes Christmas a feast that invites us in a special way to meditation, to an internal act of looking at the Word (cf. Lk 1:29; 2:19; 2:51).

◀ Melozzo da Forlì (1438–1494): The angel of the *Annunciation*.
Florence, Uffizi

I

At the Beginning of Advent:
An Advent Dialogue with the Sick

When the quiet joy of the period before Christmas makes itself felt on every side, many factors can make it especially hard to be sick. The burden of sickness prevents us from truly sharing in the joy others feel. But perhaps Advent can nevertheless become a medicine of the soul that makes it easier to bear the enforced inaction and the pain of your illness. Indeed, perhaps Advent can help us discover the unobtrusive grace that can lie in the very fact of being sick.

A very personal Advent of one's own

Let us reflect on what the word "Advent" actually means. The Latin word *adventus* can be translated

as "presence" or "arrival".[1] In the vocabulary of classical antiquity, it was a technical term for the arrival of a high official and especially for the arrival of kings or emperors in a province. It could, however, also express the arrival of a deity who emerged from hiddenness and gave proof of his presence through mighty works or of a god whose presence was solemnly celebrated in a cultic act.

The Christians adopted this word in order to express their special relationship to Jesus Christ. For Christians, he was the king who had entered

[1] On this, cf. P. Jounel in A. G. Martimort, ed., *Handbuch der Liturgiewissenschaft*, vol. 2 (Freiburg im Breisgau, 1965), pp. 266–76; on the meaning of the word *adventus*, cf. also Blaise and Chirat, *Dictionnaire latin-français des auteurs chrétiens* (Tournhout, 1954), pp. 61f.; on the history and the theology of Advent, cf. J. Pascher, *Das liturgische Jahr* (Munich, 1963), pp. 332ff.

Roger van der Weyden (ca. 1400–1464): *The Visitation*. The encounter between Mary and Elizabeth, who both expect a child. Leipzig, Museum of Fine Arts this wretched province Earth and bestowed on it the gift of his visit; and they believed that he was present in the liturgical assembly. In general terms, when they used this word, they intended to say: God is here. He has not withdrawn from the world. He has not left us alone. Although we cannot see him and take hold of him as we do with objects in this world, nevertheless he is here, and he comes to us in many ways.

Accordingly, the word *visitatio* is closely connected to the meaning of the word "Advent". This means "visit", but our ecclesiastical language has long been accustomed to translate it as "visitation". And a strange shift in our thinking has occurred here: the word "visitation" has almost completely lost the joyful contents of the word "visit". We no longer think of its original meaning; rather, we think of "visitations" as burdens and labors that we interpret as a punishment "visited upon us" by God. But the opposite ought in fact to be the case! The word "visitation" (or "visit") ought to help us perceive that even hard things may contain something of the beauty of Advent.

Just like a great joy, so too illness and suffering can be a very personal Advent of one's own—a visit by the God who enters my life and wants to encounter me personally. Even when it is difficult for us, we should at least try to understand the days of our illness in this way: The Lord has interrupted my activity for a time in order to let me be still.

In my daily living, I have little time for him and little time for myself. I am completely involved from morning to evening in all the things I have to do, and I even succeed in eluding my own grasp, because I do not know how to be alone with myself. My job possesses me; the society in which I live possesses me; entertainment of various kinds possesses me; but I do not possess myself. And this means that I gradually go to seed like an overgrown garden, first in my external activities and, then, in my inner life, too. I am propelled along by my activities, for I am merely a cog in their great machinery.

But now God has drawn me out of all this. I am obliged to be still. I am obliged to wait. I am obliged to reflect on myself; I am obliged to bear being alone. I am obliged to bear pain, and I am obliged to accept the burden of my own self. All this is hard.

But may it not be the case that God is waiting for me in this stillness? May it not be the case that he is doing here what Jesus says in the parable of the vine: "Every branch that does bear fruit he prunes, that it may bear more fruit" (Jn 15:2)?

If I learn to accept myself in these days of stillness, if I accept the pain, because the Lord is using it to purify me—does this not make me richer than if I had earned a lot of money? Has not something happened to me that is more durable and fruitful than all those things that can be counted and calculated?

A visit by the Lord—perhaps illness can present itself in a new light when we see it as a part of Advent. For when we rebel against it, this is not only because it is painful or because it is hard to be still and alone: we rebel against it because there are so many important things we ought to be doing and because illness seems meaningless. But it is not in the least meaningless! In the structure of human life as a whole, it is profoundly meaningful. It can be a moment in our life that belongs to God, a time when we are open to him and thus learn to rediscover our own selves.

Perhaps we should try an experiment. Let us understand the individual events of the day as little signs God sends us. Let us not take note only of the annoying and unpleasant things; we should endeavor to see how often God lets us feel something of his love. To keep a kind of inner diary of good things would be a beautiful and healing task.

The Lord is here. This Christian certainty is meant to help us look at the world with new eyes and to understand the "visitation" as a *visit*, as one way in which *he* can come to us and be close to us.

Paths and forms of waiting

A second basic element of Advent is *waiting*—a waiting that is an act of hope. Advent thus shows us the very essence of Christian time and the true nature of history. Jesus revealed this in many parables: in the story of the servants who are waiting

God's visit: The three angels visit Abraham and Sarah; mosaic, ca. 440.
Rome, basilica of Saint Mary Major

for the return of their master or of those other servants who forget his return and behave as if they were the proprietors; in the story of the virgins who await the bridegroom or of those other virgins who cannot wait for him; and in the parables of sowing and harvest.

In his life here on earth, man is one who waits. As a child, he wants to be an adult; as an adult, he wants to forge ahead and be successful; and finally, he yearns for rest. At last, there comes the time when he realizes that he has hoped for too little: he has set his hopes on a job and a good position, but now he has nothing else left for which to hope.

Mankind has never ceased to hope for better times; Christians hope that the Lord passes through the whole of history and that he will one day gather up all our tears and labors, so that everything will find its explanation and its fulfillment in *his* kingdom.

Nothing shows more clearly than a period of illness that man is one who waits. Every day, we wait for signs of improvement, and ultimately we wait for a complete recovery. At the same time, however, we discover that there are very different forms of waiting.

When the time is not filled with a meaningful presence, waiting becomes unbearable. When the present moment remains completely empty—when all we can do is to look for something to come, and there is nothing at all in the here and now— every second is too long. And waiting is an intolerable burden when it remains completely uncertain whether we actually dare expect anything.

But when time itself is meaningful and each moment contains something valuable of its own, the joyful anticipation of something greater, something still to come, makes even more precious that which we already experience. And it gives us a kind of invisible force that bears us across the individual moments. The Christian Advent wants to help us attain *this* kind of waiting, for this is the truly Christian form of waiting and hoping.

This is because the gifts of Jesus Christ do not belong purely to the future: they penetrate the present time, too. He is already present in a hidden manner. He speaks to me in many ways—through Sacred Scripture, through the Church year, through the saints, through many different events in my daily life, and through the whole of creation, which looks different when *he* stands behind it than when it is obscured by the mist of an uncertain origin and an uncertain future. I can speak to him; I can utter lamentations in his presence; and I can hold up my sufferings, my impatience, and my questions to him, aware that he always hears me.

If God exists, then there is no meaningless time, no time devoid of significance. Every moment has its value, even if all I can do is to endure my illness in silence. If God exists, then there is always something to hope for, even where no human voice can any longer summon me to hope. And old age and retirement are no longer the last stage of my life, a position from which all I can do is look backward: for something greater always lies ahead, and it is precisely the time of an apparent uselessness that can be the highest form of human ripening.

Christian hope does not devalue time. On the contrary, it means that every moment of life possesses its own value; it means that we can accept the present and that we ought to live it to the full, because everything we have accepted in our heart will remain.

A time of joy that no suffering can drive away

This helps us to understand a third aspect of Advent. It is not only the time of the presence and the awaiting of the Eternal God; since it is both of these, it is in a unique manner also a time

of joy, a joy that dwells within us and cannot be driven away by suffering.

Perhaps the easiest way to understand this is to look at the inner meaning of our Advent customs. Almost all of these are rooted in passages of Scripture that the Church employs in this time as words of her prayer. Here, the faithful people have, as it were, translated Scripture into visible signs.

For example, we read in Psalm 96: "Then shall all the trees of the wood sing for joy before the LORD, for he comes." The liturgy has expanded this, drawing on other texts in the Psalms, to form the following affirmation: "The mountains and hills will sing praise before God, and all the trees of the wood will clap their hands, for the Lord, the ruler, is coming to rule for ever."

The painting of Mary as *Salus Populi Romani*
Rome, basilica of Saint Mary Major

The Christmas trees we decorate are simply an attempt to make these words visible. The Lord is here—our ancestors believed this and knew this, and so the trees had to go out to meet him, they had to bow down before him, the trees themselves had to become a song of praise to their Lord. The same certainty of faith led them to make the words about the singing mountains and hills a reality. They gave a voice to the mountains, and their singing resounds down through the centuries into our own days, letting us sense something of the nearness of the Lord—for it is only he who could give men such melodies.

Even a custom like Christmas baking, apparently such an external activity, has its roots in the Church's Advent liturgy, which makes its own the glorious words of the Old Testament in these days of the declining year: "In that day, the mountains will drip sweetness, and the rivers will flow with milk and honey." People of old found in such words the embodiment of their hopes for a world redeemed. And once again, our ancestors celebrated Christmas as the day on which God truly came. When he comes at Christmas, he distributes his honey (so to speak). Truly, the earth must flow with this honey on that day: where he is present, all bitterness disappears, and there is harmony between heaven and earth, between God and man. The honey and the sweets are a sign of this peace, of concord and of joy.

This is why Christmas has become the feast when we give presents, when we imitate the God who has given his own self and has thereby given us once again that life which truly becomes a gift only when the "milk" of our existence is sweetened by the "honey" of being loved. And this love is not threatened by any death, any infidelity, or any meaninglessness.[2]

---

[2] Cf. J. Pieper, *Über die Liebe* (Munich, 1972), p. 52.

Ultimately, all this finds its unity in the joy that God has become a child who encourages us to trust as children trust and to give and receive gifts.

It may be difficult for us to accept this joyful music when we are tormented by questions, when we are afflicted both by bodily illness and psychological problems, and these would tend to make us rebel against the God whom we cannot understand. But this child is a sign of hope precisely for those who are oppressed. And this is why he has awakened an echo so pure that its consoling power can touch the hearts even of unbelievers.

Perhaps the right way to celebrate Advent is to let the signs of God's love that we receive in this period penetrate our soul, without resistance, without questions and quibbling. Warmed by these signs, we can then receive in full confidence the immeasurable kindness of this child who alone had the power to make the mountains sing and to transform the trees of the wood into a praise of God.

2

The Genealogy of Jesus

[1] *The book of the genealogy of Jesus Christ, the son of David, the son of Abraham.*

[2] *Abraham was the father of Isaac, and Isaac the father of Jacob, and Jacob the father of Judah and his brothers,*

[3] *and Judah the father of Perez and Zerah by Tamar, and Perez the father of Hezron, and Hezron the father of Ram,*

[4] *and Ram the father of Amminadab, and Amminadab the father of Nahshon, and Nahshon the father of Salmon,*

[5] *and Salmon the father of Boaz by Rahab, and Boaz the father of Obed by Ruth, and Obed the father of Jesse,*

[6] *and Jesse the father of David the king. And David was the father of Solomon by the wife of Uriah,*

[7] *and Solomon the father of Rehoboam, and Rehoboam the father of Abijah, and Abijah the father of Asa,*

[8] *and Asa the father of Jehoshaphat, and Jehoshaphat the father of Joram, and Joram the father of Uzziah,*

[9] *and Uzziah the father of Jotham, and Jotham the father of Ahaz, and Ahaz the father of Hezekiah,*

[10] *and Hezekiah the father of Manasseh, and Manasseh the father of Amos, and Amos the father of Josiah,*

[11] *and Josiah the father of Jechoniah and his brothers, at the time of the deportation to Babylon.*

[12] *And after the deportation to Babylon: Jechoniah was the father of Shealtiel, and Shealtiel the father of Zerubbabel,*

[13] *and Zerubbabel the father of Abiud, and Abiud the father of Eliakim, and Eliakim the father of Azor,*

[14] *and Azor the father of Zadok, and Zadok the father of Achim, and Achim the father of Eliud,*

[15] *and Eliud the father of Eleazar, and Eleazar the father of Matthan, and Matthan the father of Jacob,*

[16] *and Jacob the father of Joseph the husband of Mary, of whom Jesus was born, who is called Christ.*

[17] *So all the generations from Abraham to David were fourteen generations, and from David to the deportation to Babylon fourteen generations, and from the deportation to Babylon to the Christ fourteen generations.*

From chapter 1 of the Gospel according to Matthew

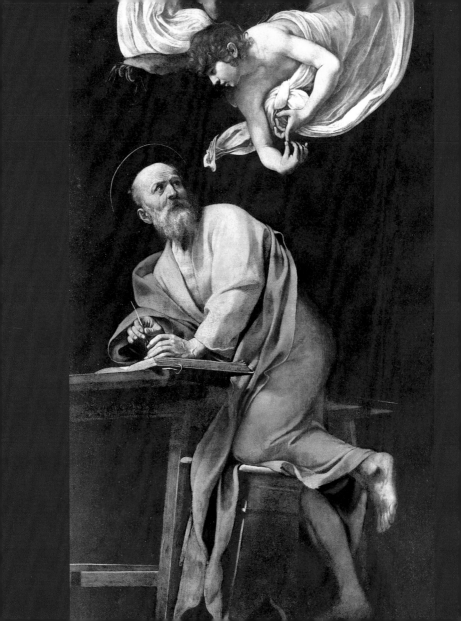

The genealogy with which Matthew begins his Gospel (1:1–17) shows us that Jesus was a man woven into a human history with its ups and downs. He was the fruit of a lengthy path; and the ultimate goal of this path was to bring forth the Christ. Since it is also the genealogy of Abraham, it teaches us something about God's faithfulness: through all the detours of human history, God keeps his promise. He does not forget the assurances he has given. God is not silent. He remains true to himself, and he knows how to open up a path for his fidelity, despite all the wrong turns taken by men. This is

Michelangelo da Caravaggio (1573–1610):
Saint Matthew and the Angel.
Rome, church of San Luigi dei Francesi

also the genealogy of David: the letters of the alphabet with which the number fourteen is written in Hebrew are the same letters we find in David's name. Thus, the genealogy is a Gospel about Christ the King, a royal fanfare: this hidden man, this crucified man, is the real king, and the entire structure of history finds its goal in him.

A genealogy for the Church of Jews and Gentiles

We must also note another point: this genealogy also mentions women, four women from Jewish history and Mary. There was indeed a tradition of emphasizing four women in the history of Israel as the great ancestresses: Sarah, Rebekah, Leah, and Rachel. However, Matthew mentions, not these four, but four others—four women who were somewhat embarrassing figures, women who disturbed the purity of a genealogy and were considered blemishes on the history of Israel. This is why people tended to pass over these women in silence.

Some scholars have suggested that Matthew is pointing in his genealogy of Jesus to something he intended to make the underlying leitmotif of his entire Gospel: that the last shall be the first. Human criteria are overturned by God. God has chosen that which is weak. And since all these four women are sinners, the mention of their names makes the genealogy a genealogy of the grace that welcomes the sinner and that is based on forgiveness, not on human greatness or achievements.[1]

---

[1] Cf., for example, G. Kittel, "Thamar", in *ThWNT* 3:1–3. Kittel understands the theological meaning of the four women entirely in the sense of grace as the justification of the sinner; but E. Schweizer, *Das Evangelium nach Matthäus*, Das Neue Testament deutsche 2, 3rd ed. (Göttingen, 1981), p. 9, has rightly perceived what I believe to be the decisive point: that the text intends to show us that the Church comes from a history on which both Jews and Gentiles have left their mark. In this way, too, the "genealogy of grace" announces the central theme of the Gospel; but here, the idea of grace is understood in a more comprehensive manner, in its relation to world history and the Church as a whole.

All this is true, but I believe that it does not do justice to the central perspective Matthew intended. If we look more closely, we will see that the sin involved in all four Old Testament narratives was the sin of a man, not the sin of a woman! The specific point about these four women is that they were not Jewish. It was precisely these Gentile women who appeared on the scene at decisive turning points in the history of Israel, and this is why they may rightly be considered the real ancestresses of the kingdom in Israel.

First of all, we have Rahab, the harlot who admitted the spies of Israel to the city of Jericho and thus opened the door into the Holy Land. She does this because she believes in the God of these foreigners, and accordingly she is regarded in the New Testament as the mother of faith and as the mother of good works (Heb 11:31; Jas 2:25). In the early Church, Rahab—the filthy harlot whose house nevertheless became the home of

Israel and the path to the occupation of the promised land—is portrayed as the type of the Church of the Gentiles. She represents the Church that came together from the filth of paganism. In her yearning for salvation, this Church opened the door to God's spies—that is, the apostles, who found nowhere to dwell in Israel—and thus permitted the whole world to become the Holy Land of faith. Her filthy lodging house became the sacred house of fellowship with Jesus Christ.

Ruth was a Gentile who married a Jew; but after his death, she was free to return to her own people. And yet she remained at a time of great distress for Israel, helping her mother-in-law in her difficult situation, because the words of her marriage ceremony had become the defining structure of Ruth's life: "Your God shall be my God." This Gentile woman had become a believer in the God of Israel, and she became the ancestress of David's dynasty.

Bathsheba, the wife of Uriah, was presumably a Hittite, like her husband. When she became the wife of David, she accepted his God, and she became the mother of Solomon, who is repeatedly presented in Matthew's Gospel as an image of Jesus Christ.

Finally, we have Tamar, whose right to have children was refused by Judah but who compelled him to grant her wish: it was through her that the kingdom came to the tribe of Judah, thereby fulfilling the promise made in Jacob's blessing: "The scepter shall not depart from Judah, nor the ruler's staff from between his feet, until he comes to whom it belongs; and to him shall be the obedience of the peoples" (Gen 49:10).

This means that the four women transform this genealogy, which at first sight is only the genealogy of Abraham and David, into a genealogy for the

Fifth-century picture of Mary.
Rome, church of Santa Francesca Romana

Church of Jews and Gentiles. It points ahead to that which is to come, namely, the Church of the peoples. Indeed, one could say that in the genealogy, these four women push aside all the tremendously important "history of men"; it is the women who are the real hinges on which the genealogy turns. Instead of a genealogy of supposedly male deeds, it becomes a genealogy of faith and of grace. The real heart of this history, the continuing story of God's promise, is based on the faith of these women.

Despite all the differences, we can see an inherent connection here to the fifth woman, in whom the genealogy reaches its culmination: Mary. At this final decisive point, we see the complete relativization and the ultimate unimportance of the whole "history of men". Up to now, the individual names are always linked by the phrase "was the father of". But at the close of the genealogy, we hear nothing about "begetting". We are told:

"Jacob was the father of Joseph, the husband of Mary, of whom Jesus was born, who is called Christ." Joseph was not the father of Jesus; he was only the husband of Mary. It is only through the bridge of this legal belonging, not by means of a biological link, that Jesus belongs to this genealogy and the genealogy to him. He is the legal and legitimate possessor of the genealogy; for Israel, the legal origin, not the biological origin, was always the decisive point, the real heart of the matter. Thanks to the bridge of this law, the Old Testament belongs to Jesus.

A new beginning through Mary's fiat

At the same time, a new beginning is made. This true beginning that determines everything takes place through faith—through Mary's *fiat*. This true beginning is prefigured and anticipated in something that

47

again and again led to an effective beginning in Israel: the faith of mothers, the faith of foreigners.

In this way, the evangelist makes accessible to us something that can seem very distant. This beginning can become a present reality at every moment, making possible a relatedness to Jesus and union with him. Mary's *fiat* is the sphere we can enter at any time, the space that this Gospel invites us to enter. Here, a beginning takes place; here, we touch the Incarnation of the Lord of which the Gospel speaks to us; here, too, we approach God's answer to the prayer in which the Church's liturgy today sums up the Gospel: the request that we men may share in the life of God, with Christ and in Christ.[2]

---

[2] This homily was preached on December 17. The Prayer of the Mass finds its starting point in the profession of faith that the Logos became incarnate in Christ from the Virgin Mary. It summarizes the essential

(cont.)

Guido Reni (1575–1642): *Saint Joseph*.
Rome, National Gallery of Ancient Art

When we enter this sphere, the entire Old Testament belongs to us with Christ. We take our place in the "holy exchange" between God and man and between man and man, in which everything belongs to everyone—that is, in the "communion of saints". The Gospel summons us to enter the door of the *fiat*. This is its invitation; this is the hand of grace that the Lord stretches out to us on this day of Advent.

---

theological contents of the genealogy and formulates this as a prayer: "May we come to share in the divinity of Christ, who humbled himself to share in our humanity."

3
The Tree of Life

A few years ago, I was fortunate enough to see the oldest surviving Christmas tree in the world, which forms a kind of reredos behind the high altar in the church at Christkindl near Steyr. The history of this tree takes us back to the year 1694. At that time, Steyr had a new sacristan and choirmaster who suffered from epilepsy—or, as the chronicle innocently puts it, "the sickness where one falls down". He came from Melk, where he had become acquainted with the devotion to the child Jesus. He placed a picture of the Holy Family in the hollow of a medium-sized pine, and he found strength and consolation as he said his prayers before this picture. Then he heard of an image of the Christ child that had healed a paralyzed nun, and after some time

Leonardo da Vinci (1452–1519): *Saint Anne, Mary, and the Child.* Paris, Louvre he succeeded in obtaining an exact copy, a waxen Christ child holding a cross in one hand and the crown of thorns in the other. He brought this image to the tree and said his prayers before it, sensing that a healing power radiated from the image.

Gradually, people heard about this, and they began to make pilgrimages to the Christ child in the tree. The Church authorities in Passau were slow to approve of this popular devotion, but the local people were finally given permission to erect a little church around this tree, and the foundation stone of the Christkindl church was laid in 1708. It was built by the most celebrated Austrian architects of the time, on the model of Santa Maria Rotonda in Rome. One might say that it has become a precious husk around the tree, out of which the altar and the tabernacle grow. The tree still bears the little waxen Christ child. He wears a crown, and rays go forth from the figure, giving an assurance of faith and hope to many people.

The rediscovered tree of life

This story is more than just an interpretation of one of our loveliest Christmas customs: I have come to see it as a key to the very heart of the mystery of Christmas itself. This tree is now the rediscovered tree of life from paradise; as an old German hymn says, "the cherub with his flaming sword no longer blocks the way." And this tree is Mary with the blessed fruit of her womb, Jesus. And Jesus is there as a child without weapons, issuing an invitation to us. He is "Immanuel", God as a child, a God to whom we may speak in intimate language. He invites us to himself—and in a very deep sense, we are all suffering from "the sickness where one falls down". Again and again, we find ourselves unable interiorly to walk upright and to stand. Again and again, we fall down; we are not masters of our own lives; we are alienated; we are not free. The rotunda of the church building underlines this. The circular octagon is the classical form of baptisteries, which in turn is linked to very ancient traditions in religious history, namely, to the cave and to the circular building that hint at the maternal womb—at the mystery of birth.

Thus, the building points once more to Mary, to the Church, and to our baptism and rebirth. The building explains to us what it means to affirm that God has become a child. It explains to us the meaning of Jesus' words to Nicodemus: "Unless one is born of water and the Spirit, he cannot enter the kingdom of God" (Jn 3:5). And another saying of Jesus belongs here too: "Unless you turn and become like children, you will never enter the kingdom of heaven" (Mt 18:3).

Martin Schongauer (ca. 1450–1491):
Madonna of the Rose Garden (1473).
Colmar, Dominican church

Karl Marx once said that a man is not independent as long as he owes his existence to the goodwill of someone else. As long as you are not autonomous, you are not free—you are dependent. This seems perfectly obvious! But if we look more closely, we discover that Marx's words declare love to be slavery. For *love* means that I need the other and that I need his goodwill.

This idea of freedom understands love as servitude; in other words, it presupposes the destruction of love. This makes it an attack on the truth of human existence, since this draws its life from love. And it is an attack on God, since man is God's image precisely by the fact that he needs love. For God, too, did not want to be "independent" of love: the Son exists only from the Father, and the Spirit exists only from the Father and the Son, and the Father exists only for the other two Persons. It is only in this mutual dependency, as the triune Deity, that he is God. And this must be so, if God is love.

The fruit from the tree of life

The child Jesus points us to this primal truth of human existence: We must be born again. We must be accepted, and we must let ourselves be accepted. We must transform our dependency into love and become free therein. We must be born again, laying aside our pride and becoming a child. In the child Jesus, we must recognize and receive the fruit of life. This is what Christmas is meant to bring about in us. This is the truth of the child, the truth of the fruit from the tree of life. The tree at Christkindl, which tells us all this, is at the same time a monstrance, the appearance of the One who is the bread of life, the appearance of salvation. And this tree is a cross—and thus has become an altar. The child bears the cross and the crown of thorns in his hands. These are the signs of the love that transforms the tree into a cross and the cross into the table of eternal life.

The true tree of life is not far from us, some-where in a world that we have lost. It has been established in our midst, not only as an image and sign, but in reality. Jesus, who is himself the fruit of the tree of life, and life itself, has become so small that our hands can enclose him. He makes himself dependent upon us in order to make us free and to raise us up from our "sickness where we fall down". Let us not disappoint the trust he places in us. Let us place ourselves in his hands, just as he has placed himself in our hands!

Stephan Lochner (ca. 1410–1451): *The Birth of Christ.* Munich, Alte Pinakothek

4

Ox and Ass at the Crib

At Christmas, our heartfelt wish is that this festive season, in the midst of all the hectic pace of contemporary life, may give us some contemplation and joy and a contact with the loving kindness of our God that will supply new courage to continue on our journey. It may be helpful to begin these brief reflections on what this feast can say to us today by looking at the origins of the Christmas celebration.

The Church's calendar developed initially, not from the perspective of the birth of Christ, but on the basis of faith in his Resurrection. This means that the primal feast of Christianity is not Christmas, but Easter; for the Resurrection gave the first impetus to the Christian faith and brought the Church into existence. This is why one very early writer, Ignatius of Antioch (who died no later than 117), could call Christians "those who no longer observe the sabbath, but live according to the day of the Lord".[1] Christian existence is a paschal existence based on the Resurrection, which is celebrated on Sunday, the weekly Easter feast. It is certain that Hippolytus of Rome, in the commentary on Daniel he wrote around 204, was the first to affirm explicitly that Jesus was born on December 25; although Bo Reicke, formerly professor of exegesis in Basel, has also pointed to the festal calendar that lies behind the chronological link made in the Gospel of Luke between the birth of John the Baptist and the birth of Jesus. This would mean that Luke himself assumes that Jesus was born on December 25, the day on which the feast of the dedication of the Temple (introduced by Judas Maccabeus in 164 B.C.) was celebrated. Hence, the

---

[1] Ignatius of Antioch, *Letter to the Magnesians* 3, 1.

date of Jesus' birth would also symbolize the fact that when he appeared as God's light in the winter night, the true dedication of the Temple—the arrival of God in the heart of this earth—took place.[2]

The Christmas of Francis of Assisi

At any rate, the feast of Christmas took on a clear shape in Christendom only in the fourth century, when it took the place of the Roman feast of the unconquered sun god and taught the faithful to understand the birth of Christ as the victory of the true light; and Bo Reicke's essay makes it clear that ancient Jewish-Christian traditions were

[2] Bo Reicke, "Jahresfeier und Zeitenwende im Judentum und Christentum der Antike", *Trierer Theologische Quartalschrift* 150 (1970): 312–34. As far as I can see, liturgical scholars have as yet paid scarcely any attention to the perspectives opened up by this essay, which overturns the existing scholarly consensus about the genesis of Christmas and Epiphany.

employed in the transmutation of a pagan celebration into a Christian solemnity.

It was, however, only in the Middle Ages that the special warmth developed that moves us so much at Christmas that it has taken a much more central place than Easter in Christian hearts. Out of his profound love for the man Jesus, "God with us", Francis of Assisi helped this new element to emerge. His first biographer, Thomas of Celano, relates in his second narrative of the saint's life: "More than any other feast, he celebrated Christmas with an indescribable joy. He said that this was the feast of feasts, for on this day God became a little child and sucked milk like all human children. Francis embraced with great tenderness and devotion the pictures of the child Jesus and stammered words of tenderness, full of compassion, in

Cimabue (before 1272–after 1302): *Saint Francis.*
Assisi, lower church of San Francesco

the way children do. On his lips, the name of Jesus was sweet as honey." [3]

This devotion led to the famous celebration of Christmas at Greccio, which may have been inspired by Francis' visits to the Holy Land and to the crib in Santa Maria Maggiore in Rome. He was moved by the desire for closeness, for reality; he wanted to experience Bethlehem really present, to have a direct experience of the joy brought by the birth of the child Jesus, and to share this with all his friends.

Celano tells us of the night of the crib in his first biography, in words that have never ceased to move his readers. At the same time, this narrative had a decisive influence on the development of the most beautiful of all the Christmas customs, the crib. We may therefore justly say that that night in Greccio gave Christendom the feast of Christmas in a

[3] II Celano, 151, 199.

completely new manner, allowing the meaning of Christmas, its special warmth and humanity, the humanity of our God, to be communicated to men's souls and giving faith a new dimension. The feast of the Resurrection had pointed to the power of God, which overcomes death and teaches us to hope in the world to come. Now, however, the defenseless love of God, his humility, and his kindness came into view: he exposes himself to us in the heart of this world and wishes to teach us a new way of living and loving in this world.

It may be helpful here to pause for a moment and reflect on the location of Greccio, this place that has a significance all its own in the history of the Christian faith. Greccio is a small town in the Rieti Valley in Umbria, not very far to the northeast of Rome where lakes and mountains give the region a special charm and a silent beauty that still move us today, especially since it is scarcely touched by the bustle of tourism. The monastery of Greccio, more than two thousand feet above sea level, has retained something of the simplicity of its origins. It has remained a modest place, like the little village that lies below it; it is surrounded by a wood, as at the time of the Poor Man of Assisi, and it invites us to rest and to contemplation. Celano writes that Francis loved the inhabitants of this place in a special way because of their poverty and simplicity and that he often came here to rest. He was also attracted by a cell that was extremely poor and remote, since there was nothing there to disturb him in his contemplation of heavenly things. Poverty—simplicity—a silence on the part of men that allowed creation to speak . . . clearly, this was what Greccio meant to the saint. So this place could become his Bethlehem, and it inscribed the mystery of Bethlehem anew in the geography of souls.

But let us return to Christmas in 1223. A nobleman named John had made the property available to Francis; Celano writes that despite his aristocratic ancestry and his prominent social position, John "took no account of nobility of blood, but rather wished to attain nobility of soul". And this was why Francis loved him.[4]

Celano tells us that this John received the grace of a miraculous vision in that night: he saw a little child lying in the manger without moving. The closeness of Saint Francis woke him from his sleep. Celano continues: "This vision truly corresponded to what happened, for up to that time, the child Jesus had in fact been lying in a slumber of forgetfulness in many hearts. Through his servant Francis, the remembrance of this child was awakened and indelibly imprinted on men's memory."[5]

---

[4] I Celano 30, 84. On the genesis of the crib, cf. Dom Gougand, "La Crèche de Noël avant Saint François d'Assise", *Revue des Sciences Religieuses* 2 (1922): 26–34.

[5] I Celano 30, 86.

This picture offers a very precise description of the new dimension that Francis gave the Christian feast of Christmas thanks to his faith, which completely penetrated the heart and the emotions: the discovery of the revelation of God in the child Jesus. It is in *this* way that God has truly become "Immanuel, God with us". There is no longer any barrier of height or distance to separate us from him: as a child, he has drawn so near to us that we can address him in intimate language without any feeling of embarrassment. We have direct access to the heart of this child, and we can become his friends.

It is in the child Jesus that we see most clearly the defenselessness of God's love. God comes without weapons, because he does not want to conquer from

Giotto di Bondone (ca. 1270–1337): *The Christmas Feast at Greccio*; a scene from the cycle devoted to Saint Francis. Assisi, upper church of San Francesco the outside but to win us over from within and to transform us from within. If anything can conquer the arrogance, the violence, and the greed of man, it is the utter vulnerability of a child: and God has taken on this vulnerability in order to conquer us in this manner and to lead us to himself.

Let us not forget that the highest title of Jesus Christ is "the Son"—the Son of God. The divine dignity is specified by means of a word that describes Jesus as a perpetual child. His existence as a child corresponds in a unique way to his divinity, which is the divinity of the "Son". And this means that his existence as a child shows us how we can come to God and to deification. This also explains the meaning of his words: "Unless you turn and become like children, you will never enter the kingdom of heaven" (Mt 18:3).

One who has not grasped the mystery of Christmas has failed to grasp the decisive element in Christianity. One who has not accepted this cannot enter the kingdom of heaven—and this is what Francis wished to recall anew to the Christians of his own day and of every succeeding generation.[6]

Ox and ass know their Lord

Francis directed that an ox and an ass should be present in the cave of Greccio on Christmas night. He had told the nobleman John: "I wish in full reality to awaken the remembrance of the child as he was born in Bethlehem and of all the hardship he had to endure in his childhood. I wish to see with my bodily eyes what it meant to lie in a manger and sleep on hay, between an ox and an ass." [7]

[6] Cf. J. Ratzinger, *Der Gott Jesu Christi* (Munich, 1976), pp. 57–61; A. Schilson, *Gott kommt als Kind* (Freiburg im Breisgau, 1977).

[7] I Celano 30, 84.

From then on, the ox and ass have had their place in every crib scene—but where do they actually come from? It is well known that the Christmas narratives of the New Testament do not mention them. When we investigate this question, we discover an important factor in all the customs associated with Christmas and, indeed, in all the Christmas and Easter piety of the Church in both liturgy and popular customs.

The ox and ass are not simply products of the pious imagination: the Church's faith in the unity of the Old and New Testaments has given them their role as an accompaniment of the Christmas event. We read in Isaiah: "The ox knows its owner, and the ass its master's crib; but Israel does not know, my people does not understand" (1:3).

◄ The Christ child in the crib with ox and ass: a detail from an antependium, Catalonia, 12th/13th century.
Solsona, Diocesan Museum

The Fathers of the Church saw in these words a prophecy that pointed ahead to the new people of God, the Church consisting of both Jews and Gentiles.[8] Before God, all men, Jews and Gentiles, were like the ox and ass, without reason or knowledge. But the child in the crib has opened their eyes so that they now recognize the voice of their Master, the voice of their Lord.

It is striking to note in the mediaeval pictures of Christmas how the artists give the two animals almost human faces and how they stand before the mystery of the child and bow down in awareness and reverence. But after all, this was only logical, since the two animals were considered the prophetical symbol for the mystery of the Church—our own mystery, since we are but oxen and asses vis-à-vis the Eternal God, oxen and asses whose

[8] J. Ziegler, "Ochs und Esel an der Krippe. Biblisch-patristische Erwägungen zu Is 1,3 und Hab 3,2 (LXX)", *Münchener Theologische Zeitschrift* 3 (1952): 385–402.

eyes are opened on Christmas night, so that they can recognize their Lord in the crib.

Who recognized him, and who failed to recognize him?

But do we really recognize him? When we place the ox and ass beside the crib, we must remember the *whole* passage in Isaiah, which is not only good news—in the sense of the promise of a future knowledge—but also a judgment pronounced on contemporary blindness. The ox and ass have knowledge, "but Israel does not know, my people does not understand."

Who is the ox and ass today, and who is "my people" without understanding? How can we recognize the ox and the ass? How can we recognize "my people"? And why does the lack of reason recognize, while reason is blind?

In order to discover the answer, we must return with the Fathers of the Church to the first Christmas. Who recognized him? And who failed to recognize him? And why was this so?

The one who failed to recognize him was Herod, who did not even understand when they told him about the child: instead, he was blinded all the more deeply by his lust for power and the accompanying paranoia (Mt 2:3). Those who failed to recognize him were "all Jerusalem with him" (ibid.). Those who failed to recognize him were the "people in soft garments"—those with a high social position (Mt 11:8). Those who failed to recognize him were the learned masters who were experts in the Bible, the specialists in biblical interpretation who admittedly knew the correct passage in Scripture but still failed to understand anything (Mt 2:6).

Those who recognized him were the "ox and the ass" (in comparison to these men of prestige): the shepherds, the Magi, Mary and Joseph. But could things have been otherwise? Those with a high social position are not in the stable where the child Jesus lies: that is where the ox and the ass have their home.

And what about us? Are we so far away from the stable because our garments are much too soft and we are much too clever? Do we get entangled to such an extent in learned exegesis of the Scriptures, in demonstrations of the inauthenticity or the historical accuracy of individual passages, that we become blind to the child himself and perceive nothing of him? Are we so much "in Jerusalem", in the palace, at home in ourselves and in our arrogance and our paranoia, that we cannot hear at night the voice of the angels and then set out to adore the child?

In this night, then, the faces of the ox and the ass look at us with a question: My people does not understand, but do *you* perceive the voice of your Lord? When we place the familiar figures in the crib scene, we ought to ask God to give our hearts the simplicity that discovers the Lord in the child—just as Francis once did in Greccio. For then we, too, might experience what Celano relates about those who took part in Midnight Mass in Greccio—and his words echo closely Saint Luke's words about the shepherds on the first Christmas night—each one went home full of joy.[9]

[9] I Celano 30, 86.

5
The New Star

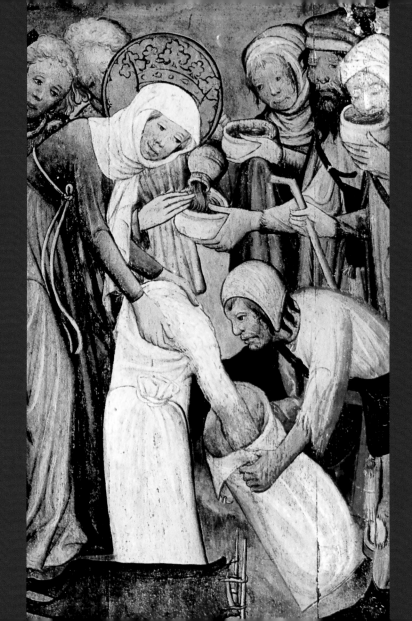

When Saint Elizabeth of Hungary lay dying on November 16, 1231, she spent her last hours telling about the life of Jesus, as she had learned to see this and understand it in the Bible and in the preaching of the Church. Toward midnight, she asked those present to be utterly silent: "Let us speak about the Savior and about the Christ child, for midnight is close at hand, when the sweet child Jesus was born."[1] In the hour of her dying, she entered the silence of Christmas night. In the night of her dying, she entered the night of light.

This shows how deeply she had imbibed the words and the realities of the faith, so that these now totally

[1] Cf. H.J. Brandt, *Elisabeth von Thüringen* (Edition Werry, 1981), p. 50.

Elizabeth of Hungary (1207–1231) distributes food to the poor. The Lubeck cycle of Saint Elizabeth, ca. 1420, painting no. 17.

filled her soul and her senses. She had allowed the history of the faith to structure the rhythm of her own time to such an extent that for Elizabeth, the hours of the day were no longer merely phases in the movements of the sun and the stars: they were hours that told the story of God's love for us.

Silence, the sphere where God is born

Saint Elizabeth asked those around her to be utterly silent, since a child was about to be born. This might seem almost playful—the child wants to sleep, and one should not disturb him! But this apparent playfulness is in reality the expression of that reverence which alone is able to open up the path to the mystery. Silence is the space of this child. Silence is the sphere where God is born. It is only when we ourselves enter the sphere of silence that we reach the point where God is born.

Thus, these words of Saint Elizabeth echo one of the earliest texts of the Christmas liturgy, which came in the course of time to inspire so many hymns: the Book of Wisdom says, "While gentle silence enveloped all things, and night in its swift course was now half gone, your all-powerful word leaped from heaven, from the royal throne, into the midst of the land that was doomed" (18:14–15).

As early as the beginning of the second Christian century, Ignatius of Antioch drew on this passage when he wrote of three mysteries that cried aloud but were hidden from the prince of this world since they had taken place in the silence of God (*Letter to the Ephesians* 19, 1).

Learning to listen in the silence

Christmas invites us into this silence of God, and his mystery remains hidden to so many people because they cannot find the silence in which God acts. How do we find it? Mere silence on its own does not suffice to create it, for a man may be silent externally while in himself he is torn this way and that by all the confusion of the world. It is possible to keep silent yet experience a terrible din within oneself.

Becoming silent means discovering a new order of things. It means that I do not limit my attention to those things I myself can produce and display to others. It means that I do not limit my interest to those things men consider important and valuable. Silence means developing the inner senses, the sense of the conscience, the sensitivity to the eternal in us, the ability to listen to God.

Scientists tell us that the dinosaurs died out because they developed in the wrong direction: a lot of armor plating and not much brain, a lot of muscles and not much understanding. Are not we, too, developing in the wrong direction: a lot of technology, but not much soul? A thick armor plating of material know-how, but a heart that has become empty? Have we not lost the ability to perceive the voice of God in us and to recognize and acknowledge the good, the beautiful, and the true?

Remaining open to God

"Let us be silent, let us speak about the Savior, for midnight is close at hand." Is it not high time to do what Saint Elizabeth tells us? Is it not high time to correct the course that our "evolution" is taking?

Such a correction cannot consist in a foolish renunciation of human work and the cultivation of the earth. Rather, it means giving renewed space to the ethical and religious reason in man.

The silence that faith requires means that man is not so completely absorbed by the system of the economic-technological civilization that he is reduced to one function within this system. We must learn anew to grasp that there is something lying between science and superstition: that deeper ethical and religious insight which alone can banish superstition and make man human by seeing him in the light of God.

Christmas is meant to help us achieve this correction of our course, thereby performing for one another and for the world the service that is so urgently needed. For the deepest distress of men today is not due to the crisis of our material resources; the problem is that the windows that give access to God have been bricked up, and we are consequently at risk of losing the air our heart breathes, the core of human freedom and dignity.

Receiving light and giving light

Let us return to Saint Elizabeth. Her last words were: "Then he created a new star, which had never shone before." [2] As she looked at this star, she passed away. The star she had followed throughout her life shone for her in her last hour, too, on her last path, which thus became a path into light.

The star of Christmas night—this is, first of all, the incarnate Son himself. He is the light that shows the path through the streets of history. He shatters the superstition that blooms all the more exuberantly as faith disintegrates. He shows the absurdity of the astrology that wishes to imprison man in the straitjacket of unending cycles of constellations, cycles in which there is nothing new, but only the repetition of something that never changes.

[2] Ibid.

Man's true constellations are those men who show him the new path of his heart and his vocation. Christ is the star that has risen for us. In faith, he himself kindles for us the light that makes other men stars who show the way to him. Elizabeth became such a star. And this is why we pray in the second Mass of Christmas: "May the light of faith shine in our words and actions."

This makes Christmas a very practical matter. To look at the star means receiving light and giving light, radiating in the world around us the light that we have received, so that it can provide orientation to others, too. We have more than enough opportunities to do this, even outside Advent: once our heart has awakened, we see around us so many others who are waiting for a light. Let them not call out to us in vain.

One of the three Wise Men points to the star: detail from an altar, Catalonia, ca. 1200.
Barcelona, Museum of Art of Catalonia

6

"The Light Shines in the Darkness"

[8] *And in that region there were shepherds out in the field, keeping watch over their flock by night.*

[9] *And an angel of the Lord appeared to them, and the glory of the Lord shone around them, and they were filled with fear.*

[10] *And the angel said to them, "Be not afraid; for behold, I bring you good news of a great joy which will come to all the people;*

[11] *for to you is born this day in the city of David a Savior, who is Christ the Lord.*

[12] *And this will be a sign for you: you will find a baby wrapped in swaddling cloths and lying in a manger."*

[13] *And suddenly there was with the angel a multitude of the heavenly host praising God and saying,*

[14] *"Glory to God in the highest, and on earth peace among men with whom he is pleased!"*

[15] *When the angels went away from them into heaven, the shepherds said to one another, "Let us go over to Bethlehem and see this thing that has happened, which the Lord has made known to us."*

[16] *And they went with haste, and found Mary and Joseph, and the baby lying in a manger.*

[17] *And when they saw it they made known the saying which had been told them concerning this child;*

[18] *and all who heard it wondered at what the shepherds told them.*

[19] *But Mary kept all these things, pondering them in her heart.*

[20] *And the shepherds returned, glorifying and praising God for all they had heard and seen, as it had been told them.*

From chapter 2 of the Gospel according to Luke

The first Christmas hymn in history, which established for all time the inner melody of Christmas, was not composed by men. Saint Luke transmits it to us as the song of the angels who were the "evangelists" of Christmas night: "Glory to God in the highest, and on earth peace among men"—the men who enjoy his favor, the men of good will.

A peace that comes from the glory of God

This hymn lays down a criterion. It helps us to understand what Christmas is really about. It contains a word that moves people today more than any other single word: *peace*. The biblical word *shalôm*, which we translate in this way, means much more than the mere absence of war: it tells us that human affairs are as they should be, it denotes well-being, a world in which trust and brotherhood rule, a world without fear or deprivation or cunning or falsehood. Peace on earth—that is the goal of Christmas. But the angels' song speaks first of a principle without which there cannot be any lasting peace: the glory of God. This is what Bethlehem teaches us about peace: peace among men comes from the glory of God. If we are concerned about men and their well-being, we must first of all be concerned about the glory of God. The glory of God is not a private matter left to the arbitrary whim of the individual; it is a matter of public concern. It is a common good, and where God is not honored among men, man too cannot be honored. *This* is why Christmas is about peace among men: thanks to Christmas, the glory of God has been reestablished in a new way among men.

The new time of peace

From the very beginning, this was made clear by the date of this feast. In the Jewish calendar, December 25 was and remains the feast of Hanukkah, the feast of lights, which recalls how on this day in 165 B.C., Judas Maccabeus removed the altar of Zeus—which tradition called the "abomination of desolation in the holy place"—from the Temple in Jerusalem. It was on the same date that the Syrian King Antiochus, who was worshipped as "Zeus", had set up the pagan idol in the Temple, designating December 25 as his own feast day. Now it became the date of the cleansing of the Temple, the day on which the glory of God, which had been trampled underfoot, was reestablished and God began to be honored anew in the proper manner. It was from this day on that Israel dated its own rebirth: as soon as it was once again able to serve God in the appropriate way, Israel itself was restored.

VICTOR CARPATHIVS
· M · D · X ·

Since the week from December 25 to 31 was also the week before the New Year, this restoration took on an even deeper significance. It portrayed the new beginning of creation, the new time of freedom for which men hoped. This is why, as early as around 100 B.C., the birth of the messianic child was expected on this date. People hoped that the Messiah would teach them how to honor God aright and that he would thereby initiate the new time of freedom. During Jesus' own lifetime, this feast was already celebrated as the feast of lights, in keeping with the prophet Isaiah's words: "The people who walked in darkness have seen a great light" (9:2).[1]

---

[1] On the connection between Christmas and the Jewish feast of the dedication of the temple (Hanukkah), cf. Bo Reicke, "Jahresfeier und Zeitenwende im Judentum und Christentum der Antike", *Trierer Theologische Quartalschrift* 150 (1970): 312–34.

Vittore Carpaccio (1455/1456–1525/1526): An angel playing a lute. Venice, Gallery of the Academy

In his infancy narrative, Luke unfolds a chronology with a profound symbolic meaning, dating it in such a way that the birth of Jesus occurs during the feast of Hanukkah, on the night of lights, which thus became the Christian feast of Christmas.[2] All he seeks to do here is to offer a further exegesis of the song of the angels: In his birth, Christ has truly done what Judas Maccabeus sought in vain to do. Christ has banished the pagan idols from the world. He has constructed the temple of his body. He has reestablished the glory of God.

All the terrible events of world history seem to constitute a grave accusation against God. But when God appears before us, unarmed, with his love as his only might, all the frightening images of God lose their plausibility. The human existence of the Son is the glory of the Father. In the crib and on the Cross, the glory of God is raised aloft in this world. And wherever men follow this God, a new

[2] Cf. ibid., pp. 330f.

humanity begins, and peace on earth begins, even if only in a fragmentary fashion.

The feast of Hanukkah was a day on which public worship was reformed and, hence, a feast of lights. The birth of Jesus is the true reform of worship, and all our own attempts at liturgical reform must ultimately aim to correspond to *this* reform, this true new beginning. Our goal must be to see God honored in our own human existence and in our country. There is so much in our society that could be called an "abomination of desolation"! In the false idols of pornography and in the desecration of the human person by violence, man and God are both alike dishonored—dishonored in that forgetfulness of God which is the worst form of thoughtlessness.

Men of peace

We must however also ask the positive question: How can God be honored, and how can we serve

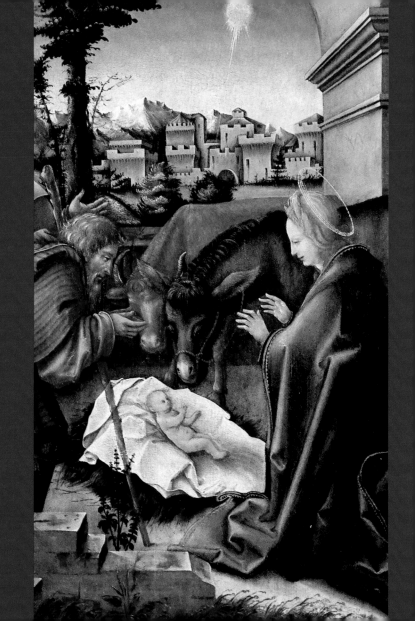

the cause of peace by doing so? The biblical narrative shows us this by telling us about those who were summoned to the crib. In their own ways, they are all men of prayer, righteous men who were devoted to the Temple.

First of all, we have Mary, whom Luke depicts as the embodiment of the contemplative. Then we have Joseph, whom Matthew calls the "righteous man"—a term that is to be understood, not in the sense of a mere legalistic righteousness that seeks to enforce its own interests, but rather in the sense of that righteousness in the heart of a man which can truly hear and see. Then we have the shepherds, in the simplicity of their hearts; the wise men, who are looking for the true Lord of the earth; and Simeon and Anna, whose lives are so closely linked to the Temple. In all their lives,

Hans Burgkmair the Elder (1473–1531):
Adoration of the Child.

God plays a decisive role, and this is why they are men of peace.

What are we to bring you?

Our picture of Christmas includes yet another element, namely, the giving of gifts. The Christmas plays our children stage in school show in great detail how the shepherds ponder what gift they can offer the newborn king—and the ideas they come up with are drawn directly from the daily lives of people in our own society today.

A liturgical hymn of the Eastern Church explores the same theme but gives it greater depth: "What can we offer you, O Christ, for having been born for us on earth as a Man? Each creature, the work of your hands, offers you a sign of gratitude: the angels, their hymn; the heavens, the star; the Magi, their gifts; the shepherds, their admiration; the earth, the cave; the desert, the manger; and all mankind, we offer you a virgin mother."[3]

Mary is the gift of mankind to Christ. And this in turn means that the Lord does not want some *thing* from man, but man himself. God does not want a certain percentage of us. He wants our heart; indeed, he wants our whole being. He wants our faith and the life that is based on faith. And from this life, he wants those gifts of which he will speak at the Last Judgment: food and clothing for the poor, compassion and mutual love, a word that gives consolation, and a presence that brings comfort to the persecuted, the imprisoned, the abandoned, and the lost.

What can we offer you, O Christ? We certainly offer him too little if all we do is to exchange costly presents with one another, gifts that are not

---

[3] *Sticharion* of Christmas: cf. P. Evdokimov, *The Art of the Icon: A Theology of Beauty*, trans. by Fr. Steven Bigham (Redondo Beach, Calif.: Oakwood Publications, 1990), p. 284.

the expression of our own selves and of a gratitude that otherwise remains silent. Let us try to offer him our faith and our own selves, even if only in the form of the prayer: "I believe, Lord, help my unbelief!" And on this day, let us not forget the many in whom he suffers on earth.

A constantly recurring drama

The Christmas icon of the Eastern Churches received its basic form as early as the fourth century. It captures the entire mystery of Christmas[4] and shows the profound connection between Christmas and Easter, the crib and Cross. Here we see the harmony of the Old and New Testaments and the harmony between heaven and earth in the song of the angels and the service of the

---

[4] Evdokimov offers a fascinating interpretation of the wide-reaching theology of the Christmas icon: ibid., pp. 269–87.

shepherds. Every figure in the icon has its own deep and enigmatic significance.

Saint Joseph is given a very strange function in this icon. He sits to the side, deep in thought. The tempter stands before him, in the garments of a shepherd. In the liturgical texts, the tempter says: "An old man like you cannot beget children or a virgin give birth any more than this staff . . . can burst into flower."[5] The liturgy tells us that a storm of contradictory thoughts raged in Joseph's heart, and he was perplexed; but enlightened by the Holy Spirit, he sang: "Alleluia!" In the figure of Saint Joseph, the icon portrays a constantly recurring drama—our own drama.

This always takes the same form: again and again, the tempter tells us that only the visible world exists. There is no Incarnation of God, and the Virgin does not give birth. These affirmations deny that God

[5] Ibid., p. 284.

knows us, that he loves us, and that he is capable of acting in this world. On the deepest level, therefore, this is a denial of the glory of God. And this is the typical temptation of our own age, which is put forward with so many clever and apparently quite new reasons that it seems incontrovertible. And yet it is always the same old temptation.

Let us ask God in his kindness to send the light of the Holy Spirit to our hearts, too. And let us ask him to permit us to leave behind the rigidity of our intellectual reflections, so that we may see his light with great joy and may sing: "Alleluia! Christ is truly born; God has become man." Let us ask him to realize in us, too, the words of the Eastern liturgy: "We offer you a virgin mother." We bring you our own selves, something more valuable than any gift of money: we bring the wealth of the true faith to you, the God and Savior of our souls.

7

"And the Word Became Flesh"

[1] *In the beginning was the Word, and the Word was with God, and the Word was God.*

[2] *He was in the beginning with God;*

[3] *all things were made through him, and without him was not anything made that was made.*

[4] *In him was life, and the life was the light of men.*

[5] *The light shines in the darkness, and the darkness has not overcome it.*

[6] *There was a man sent from God, whose name was John.*

[7] *He came for testimony, to bear witness to the light, that all might believe through him.*

[8] *He was not the light, but came to bear witness to the light.*

[9] *The true light that enlightens every man was coming into the world.*

[10] *He was in the world, and the world was made through him, yet the world knew him not.*

[11] *He came to his own home, and his own people received him not.*

[12] *But to all who received him, who believed in his name, he gave power to become children of God;*

[13] *who were born, not of blood nor of the will of the flesh nor of the will of man, but of God.*

[14] *And the Word became flesh and dwelt among us, full of grace and truth; we have beheld his glory, glory as of the only-begotten Son from the Father.*

[15] *(John bore witness to him, and cried, "This was he of whom I said, 'He who comes after me ranks before me, for he was before me.'")*

[16] *And from his fulness have we all received, grace upon grace.*

[17] *For the law was given through Moses; grace and truth came through Jesus Christ.*

[18] *No one has ever seen God; the only-begotten Son, he who is in the bosom of the Father, he has made him known.*

Prologue to chapter 1 of the Gospel according to John

In the Gospel of the third Christmas Mass (Jn 1:1–18), the lovable and familiar elements of the story of Jesus Christ's birth in the stable of Bethlehem seem to have been caught up into the foreign immensity of the mystery. We do not hear about the child and his mother or about the shepherds and their sheep or about the song of the angels that proclaims to men the peace that comes from God's glory.

And yet, there are common elements. This Gospel, too, speaks of the light that shines in the darkness; it speaks of the glory of God, which we can see as "grace" in the incarnate Word; and it speaks of the Lord who was not welcomed in his own home.

And so, through the great, mysterious words, we suddenly see the stable in which the Son of

David had to be born because there was no room for him in his own city.

If we listen more closely, we can perceive that the Gospel of the Mass on Christmas Day is telling exactly the same story as the Gospel on Christmas night—and we see that all the evangelists are relating one and the same Gospel, approaching it from various angles.

Luke and Matthew relate the earthly story, on the basis of which they allow us to see God's hidden action; John, the eagle, looks from the vantage point of the mystery of God and shows how this mystery penetrates the stable and enters the flesh and blood of man. What, then, does he wish to tell us? And what does the Church intend to tell us about Christmas Day and (on the basis of this feast) about the entire year and, indeed, about

Jacob Jordaens (1593–1673): *The Four Evangelists.*
Paris, Louvre

our life as a whole when she presents us with this solemn and hieratic text—although we might have expected the warm words of the story of Jesus' birth?

Yes, my life has a meaning!—Is that possible?

This Gospel belongs from the earliest centuries to the Christmas liturgy because it contains the sentence that expresses the very reason for our joy and the real contents of this feast: "The Word became flesh and dwelt among us" (1:14).

What we are celebrating at Christmas is not the birthday of some great man or other—and there are many great men! Nor are we simply celebrating the mystery of what it is to be a child.

It is of course true that the freshness, the purity, and the openness of a child give us hope. We find the courage to trust that new possibilities lie ahead of man. But if we cling too tightly to this aspect alone, seeing nothing more than the new beginning of life in a child, we risk ending up disillusioned and sad—for this newness, too, will be used up. The newborn child will be entangled in the competitive clash of life, and he will not be spared the compromises and humiliations that are inseparable from this struggle. And at the end, he will be a prey of death, like us all.

If all we had to celebrate was the idyll of a birth and a childhood, we would in the last analysis have no idyll at all. All that would remain would be the perennial cycle of death and birth, and one may ask whether in that case, being born is not in fact rather a cause for sadness—since it leads only to death. This is why it is so important to realize that something more has happened here: the Word has become flesh.

One of our oldest German Christmas carols sings: "This child is God's own Son." Here, something utterly immense, something we could never have thought up for ourselves—and yet, something that was always awaited, something necessary—has happened: God has become one of us. He has united himself to a human being so inseparably that this man is genuinely God from God and light from light, while remaining a true man.

The eternal meaning of the world has come to us in so real a manner that we can touch him and see him (cf. 1 Jn 1:1). For what John calls "the Word" also means in Greek "the meaning". Accordingly, we could perfectly well translate: "The meaning became flesh."

But this meaning is not simply a general idea that is inherent in the world. The meaning addresses us: the meaning is a word spoken to us. The meaning knows us; it calls to us; it leads us. The meaning

Matthias Grünewald (1470/1480–1528): *The Annunciation*, from the Isenheim altar.
Colmar, Museum Unterlinden

is not a universal law in which we play some kind of role. It is meant personally for each individual. The meaning is itself a person: the Son of the living God, who was born in a stable in Bethlehem.

Many people—indeed, in some sense, all of us—find this too good to be true. We are told: Yes, there is a meaning, and this meaning is not a powerless revolt against meaninglessness. The meaning has power. It is God. And God is good. God is not some remote highest being, forever inaccessible. He is very close to us; we can call to him; we can always reach him. He has time for me—so much time that he lay as a man in the crib and remains a man for all eternity.

Our invariable response is a doubt: Can this be true? Is it really possible for God to be a child? We are reluctant to believe that the truth is beautiful, for in our experience, the truth usually turns out to be cruel and dirty; and where this initially seems not to be the case, we dig and dig until our assumption turns out to be correct.

In the past, it was said that art serves beauty and that beauty itself is *splendor veritatis*, the splendor of the truth, its radiance from within. Today, however, many artists see their main task as unmasking man and showing that he is filthy and disgusting.

When we consider the dramas of Bertolt Brecht, we see that the author dedicates his entire genius to uncovering the truth—but no longer in order to show the radiance of the truth, but rather in order to demonstrate that the truth is dirty and that dirt is the truth. The encounter with the truth no longer ennobles: it degrades. This is why people mock Christmas and pour scorn on our joy.

We must, of course, agree that if God does not exist, then there is no light. All that remains is dirty earth. And that is the genuinely tragic truth of such works of art and literature.

"His own people received him not" (1:11). Ultimately, we prefer our defiant despair to the kindness of God, which reveals itself in Bethlehem and seeks to touch our heart. Ultimately, we are too proud to let ourselves be redeemed.

"His own people received him not." The abyss contained in these words goes far beyond the story of Mary and Joseph looking for lodgings in Bethlehem (a story that our children's Christmas plays depict every year). This abyss goes far beyond the moral appeal to think of the homeless in today's world and in our modern cities—important as this appeal undoubtedly is. These words of Saint John touch something deeper in us: the real reason why so many people in the world are homeless. Our

Raphael (1483–1520): *Mary and Elizabeth.*
Madrid, Prado

arrogance closes the door on God and, therefore, on our fellow men.

We are too proud to see God. We are like Herod and his theological specialists: on this level, we no longer hear the angels singing. On this level, we may find God either threatening or boring—but nothing more than that! On this level, we no longer want to be "his own possession"—that is, God's possession. All we want is to belong to our own selves. And this is why we cannot receive the one who comes into his own property, for that would oblige us to make a radical change and acknowledge that *he* possesses us.

He came as a child, in order to break down our pride. Perhaps we would have capitulated before power or wisdom . . . , but he does not want our capitulation: he wants our love. He wants to free us from our pride and, thus, to make us truly free.

Let us then allow the joy of this day to penetrate our souls. It is no illusion. It is the truth.

For the truth—the ultimate and genuine truth—is beautiful. And it is good. When men encounter it, they become good. The truth speaks to us in the child who is God's own Son.

His glory—in this world

Our Gospel closes with the words: "We have beheld his glory . . ." (1:14). These could be the words of the shepherds as they return from the stable and sum up what they have experienced. These could be the words in which Mary and Joseph describe their memory of the night in Bethlehem. Here, it is the disciple who looks back and tells us what happened to him when he encountered Jesus.

As Christians, we ought really all to be able to say: "We have beheld his glory." Indeed, these words explain what believing means: it means seeing his glory in this world.

One who believes sees. But have we seen? Is it not rather the case that we have remained blind? Do we ever see anything other than ourselves alone and our reflection? If we are to see something outside ourselves, it must find a correspondence within ourselves.

Let us therefore allow the mystery of this day to open our eyes and make us see. For then we will automatically live as men who have the gift of sight, as men who do not think only of themselves and do not know only themselves. The *Adveniat* collection for the needy that is taken up in Germany in Advent could be one little response to the summons addressed to us by Christmas, a sign that we have learned to hear and see and that we acknowledge God as the true owner of our own possessions. And so we, too, can become

The Birth of Christ.
Painting by a master from Central Rhineland, ca. 1480.

bearers of the light that comes from Bethlehem. Then we can pray, full of confidence: *Adveniat regnum tuum.* Your kingdom come! Your light come! Your peace come!

Pinturicchio (1454–1513): Mary (detail from *The Birth of Christ—Adoration*).
Rome, church of Santa Maria del Popolo

Note on the First Publication of the Meditations

The texts by Joseph Cardinal Ratzinger (now Pope Benedict XVI) that are presented in this book are taken from the following two volumes:

(1A): Joseph Ratzinger, *Licht, das uns leuchtet: Besinnung zu Advent und Weihnachten* (with a meditation by Pope John Paul I) (Freiburg, Basel, and Vienna: Verlag Herder, 1978).

(1B): The texts by Cardinal Ratzinger were republished in a gift edition: *Licht, das uns leuchtet: Meditationen zur Advents- und Weihnachtszeit* (Freiburg, Basel, and Vienna: Verlag Herder, 1999).

(2) Joseph Ratzinger and Heinrich Schlier, *Lob der Weihnacht* (Freiburg, Basel, and Vienna: Verlag Herder, 1982).

1. "Am Anfang des Advent—Ein Adventsgespräch mit Kranken" (At the Beginning of Advent:

An Advent Dialogue with the Sick): 1A, pp. 9–23; 1B, pp. 4–10.

2. "Der Stammbaum Jesu" (The Genealogy of Jesus): 2, pp. 7–16.

3. "Der Baum des Lebens" (The Tree of Life): 2, pp. 17–24.

4. "Ochs und Esel an der Krippe" (Ox and Ass at the Crib): 1A, pp. 25–37; 1B, pp. 11–17; translated here from the slightly expanded version in: Joseph Ratzinger, *Bilder der Hoffnung: Wanderungen im Kirchenjahr* (Freiburg, Basel, and Vienna: Verlag Herder, 1997), pp. 17–24.

5. "Der neue Stern" (The New Star): 2, pp. 25–34.

6. "Das Licht leuchtet in der Finsternis" (The Light Shines in the Darkness): 2, pp. 35–46.

7. "Und das Wort ist Fleisch geworden: Eine Weihnachtspredigt" (And the Word Became Flesh: A Christmas Homily): 1A, pp. 39–49; 1B, pp. 18–22.